Second Grade Writing Prompts for Seasons:
A Creative Writing Workbook

Bryan Cohen

Edited by Ashley Daoust.

DEDICATION

I dedicate this book to my hometown of Dresher, Pennsylvania, which thankfully has a healthy dose of all four seasons.

CONTENTS

INTRODUCTION

Welcome to the *Writing Prompts for Seasons* workbook series! Within these pages you'll find 200 writing prompts, two on each page, that will stimulate the imagination of your students or children. I've found that the key to allowing students to fully latch onto an idea is to give them a scenario followed by a question. In answering the question, young writers can take the same prompt a million different directions. You may even want to try photocopying a page and have your writers take on the same prompt at the beginning and the end of a school year, just to see how different their storytelling has become.

The *Writing Prompts for Seasons* series is a collection of books I've created after seeing how many parents and teachers have visited my website, Build Creative Writing Ideas (located at http://www.build creative-writing-ideas.com). The most popular pages on my site coincide with prompts about the four seasons of spring, summer, fall and winter. I imagine this means two things: teachers and parents are searching for seasonal writing activities, and children enjoy writing about the changing weather and the upcoming holidays. I hope that this series will meet both of those needs while inspiring creativity in the minds of our youth. The five books in the series are available for grades 1, 2, 3, 4 and 5. The prompts become more complex with each volume, but continue to remain imaginative and creative throughout.

I love hearing about the progress of students on my site and I'm always interested in hearing new ideas for delivering creative writing prompts to writers from the ages of 5 to 105. Feel free to contact me on my website with any questions and comments you can think of. I hope you and your future best-selling authors thoroughly enjoy this and other books in the series. Happy writing!

Sincerely,
Bryan Cohen
Author of *Writing Prompts for Seasons*

PS: While there is space below each prompt for your budding writers to write, there is a good chance they may have more to say than they can fit on the page. There is an extra page in the back if you'd like to photocopy it, but I strongly suggest that you also get a notebook and some extra pencils just in case. A dictionary for challenging words may also be helpful.

Name _____ Date _____

1. Describe what it feels like to bite into a juicy slice of watermelon on a hot summer's day. How does it make you feel and why?

_____

_____

_____

_____

_____

2. Your family has given you permission to pick all of the foods you want to cook during a neighborhood barbecue. What foods do you put on the menu and why? How do the guests enjoy your food selection?

_____

_____

_____

_____

_____

Name _____ Date _____

3. There are many different sources and varieties of lemonade
including lemonade from a mix, in a can, and freshly squeezed. What is your favorite kind
of lemonade and why? If you were running a lemonade stand, would you use that kind?
Why or why not?

_____

_____

_____

_____

4. Imagine that you have just gotten a new job creating new summer ice cream flavors.
What are some of the ideas you might come up with? Which would you enjoy eating the
most and why?

_____

_____

_____

_____

Name _____ Date _____

5. Eating that corn on the cob didn't start with your parents putting it
in the oven. Trace the steps of where the corn came from, including the grocery store, the
farmer, and the people who drove it there. How is the corn's story similar to the stories of
other foods you eat?

_____

_____

_____

_____

6. What fresh fruits would you put into a summer fruit smoothie? What benefits might you
get from eating so much real fruit? Would you add sugar or anything else to it? Why or
why not?

_____

_____

_____

_____

Name _____ Date _____

7. Cotton candy is a delicious summer carnival treat, but the candy's texture is so strange it's almost as if the tasty treat is from another planet. Imagine that cotton candy was from outer space. Where would it have come from and how did it get here?

_____

_____

_____

_____

8. Describe a trip through the local farmer's market to buy fresh vegetables and herbs with your family. What do you enjoy about the market and why? What don't you enjoy and why don't you like it?

_____

_____

_____

_____

Name _____ Date _____

9. One of the best parts of visiting the local pool or beach is the chance to get what you want from the snack bar. What are some of your favorite snack bar choices? If you had the choice between a tasty snack bar treat or something fresh from the ocean, which would you rather have and why?

_____

_____

_____

_____

_____

10. Different parts of the world have different summer foods, ranging from fried county fair desserts to salty seafood. What would you consider to be a summer delicacy in your area? If you could choose one place in the world to visit just because of the food, where would it be and why?

_____

_____

_____

_____

Name _____ Date _____

11. While floating in the ocean, you see a big jellyfish just a few feet
away! What is your next step? What would you do if you got stung and why?

_____

_____

_____

_____

12. Imagine that you are a tiny hummingbird drinking from a feeder in a beautiful garden.
What would it be like to fly around so fast? What might be some dangers you would face
on a daily basis? Where would you live and why?

_____

_____

_____

_____

Name _____ Date _____

13. Upon visiting a desert village, your family has decided to ride camels into town. What might it be like to sit atop this humped creature while moving through the sand? Would you be scared? Why or why not?

_____

_____

_____

_____

14. Summer is a wonderful time to visit the animals at the zoo. Which is your favorite animal to watch while walking through the zoo and why? What would it be like to share a cage with him or her? What would you do together and why?

_____

_____

_____

_____

Name _____ Date _____

15. Imagine that all humans had necks as long and tall as those of giraffes. How would our lives be different? What different kinds of clothes might we need to create? Would it be better to have our regular necks or giraffe necks and why?

_____

_____

_____

_____

16. Create a conversation between two tropical birds watching a safari of tourists taking pictures. What might the two birds have to say about the strange-looking humans and why?

_____

_____

_____

_____

Name _____ Date _____

17. There you are at the starting line, ready to race against a cheetah.
Do you think you'd stand a chance? Why or why not? Would your chances improve if you had a bike or a car? Why or why not?

_____

_____

_____

_____

_____

18. If you live in a warm enough climate, you likely have gnats and mosquitoes to deal with during the nights of summer. What are some dangers of these insects? What are some of the ways to avoid being bitten?

_____

_____

_____

_____

Name _____ Date _____

19. Some kinds of birds and elephants can have a symbiotic relationship, as the birds can get a meal from the back of an elephant and the elephants can be pest free. Do you have a symbiotic relationship with anyone in your life? If so, who is it and how do you benefit each other? If not, imagine life as one of these elephant-friendly birds and write about your day.

_____

_____

_____

_____

_____

20. The animals of summer can be very different from town to town. What are some of summer animals in your area and how do they interact with humans?

_____

_____

_____

_____

Name _____ Date _____

21. Plants like cacti and succulents survive summer by storing the
water they take in. Imagine that you looked and acted like a cactus when it came to storing
liquid and being prickly. What sorts of things wouldn't you be able to do? What benefits
might there be to the cactus lifestyle?

_____

_____

_____

_____

_____

22. Perennials, plants that live for two or more years, may go to sleep during the summer to
avoid the scorching temperatures. What would your parents do if you decided not to leave
your room or do anything of value all summer long? Would you get bored?

_____

_____

_____

_____

Name _____ Date _____

23. You've been challenged to a pepper-eating contest. The person to
eat the most summer peppers without drinking water is the winner. Would you take up that
challenge? If so, what would your secret weapon be for winning? If not, who that you
know might be willing?

_____

_____

_____

_____

24. Certain plants like yarrow flowers, Russian sage, and frostweed, thrive with low
amounts of water and might actually die with too much. What does it mean to have too
much of a good thing? Has that ever happened to you? If so, explain what occurred, and if
not, what might you overindulge in and why?

_____

_____

_____

_____

Name _____ Date _____

25. Tomatoes, which are grown during the summer, used to be thrown at performers who told bad jokes back in the nineteenth century. Have you ever seen a show, live or on television, that might have deserved some tomatoes heaved its way? What was so bad about it?

_____

_____

_____

_____

_____

26. To make some extra money over the summer, you've started your own landscaping business. What would it be like to have to cut dozens of lawns every day? What would you think about while riding your mower to pass the time? Would you enjoy the work? Why or why not?

_____

_____

_____

_____

Name _____ Date _____

27. Avocados, the primary ingredient in guacamole, are a delicious summer treat despite being green. Have you ever assumed something would taste different because of how it looked on the outside? Do you think the same kind of thing could happen with a person? Why or why not?

_____

_____

_____

_____

28. Your family has moved to the countryside to begin creating grape and berry juices by stomping on the fruits from sunrise to sunset. Describe what it might feel like to squish the grapes and berries underneath your toes. Would you enjoy it? Why or why not?

_____

_____

_____

_____

Name _____ Date _____

29. What do the plants in your area smell like? How do they smell different from plants during other seasons and why?

_____

_____

_____

_____

_____

30. Create a conversation between a summer plant and a summer animal. How would they be enjoying the toastiest season and why?

_____

_____

_____

_____

_____

Name _____ Date _____

31. The tilting of the Earth gives the Northern Hemisphere its most daytime hours of the entire year. What are some of the ways that you take advantage of having more daylight? What are the pros and cons of having more daylight?

_____

_____

_____

_____

_____

32. A particle of sand that you pick up on the beach could be from thousands of miles away. Imagine the journey of that single grain of sand. How do you think the sand ended up where you might be sitting during your summer vacation?

_____

_____

_____

_____

Name _____ Date _____

33. Waves in the ocean can be caused by storms that are thousands of miles away. What are some of the things that you enjoy doing on a summer wave? Would you rather experience waves in a controlled wave pool or in the ocean and why?

_____

_____

_____

_____

_____

34. The largest sand castle in the world was over 30 feet tall and took more than 100 truckloads of sand. Imagine that you and some friends were trying to beat the record. What would your massive castle look like and how would you succeed?

_____

_____

_____

_____

Name _____ Date _____

35. Summer is a season full of thunderstorms and lighting. Lightning results from friction in the air and a difference in electrical charge between the sky and the ground. Are you afraid of lightning? Why or why not? Why is it important to be safe during a storm?

_____

_____

_____

_____

36. Coral reefs are important near a tropical island because they keep the waves from damaging the beach. Scientists have created artificial reefs by intentionally sinking ships that the coral and fish can live inside. Do you think a fish would realize it's living inside a boat as opposed to the natural ocean? Why or why not?

_____

_____

_____

_____

Name _____ Date _____

37. Sunburns, a summer fixture, are caused when ultraviolet light
penetrates through the atmosphere and causes damage to your skin. What are some ways to prevent sunburn from happening? Why is it important to protect yourself even if you have a tan?

_____

_____

_____

_____

_____

38. Sweat may be a bit gross but it's necessary to keep yourself cool. Think back to the sweatiest you've ever been. What caused you to sweat so much? How did you feel afterwards and why?

_____

_____

_____

_____

Name _____ Date _____

39. Ice cream headaches or brain freezes are caused when the nerves
above the roof of your mouth get too cold. Have you ever eaten a lot more ice cream than
you should? If so, what flavor was it and what happened afterwards? If not, why do you
think it's important to eat dessert in moderation?

_____

_____

_____

_____

40. Fireflies are known for lighting up the night sky during the summer. These beetles use
the process of bioluminescence to either find a mate or find another firefly they want to
eat. If you could light up at night, what would you use your ability for and why?

_____

_____

_____

_____

Name _____ Date _____

41. What is your most memorable summer experience? Why does
this memory stick out so much? What could have made it even more distinct and why?

_____

_____

_____

_____

_____

42. As you get older, what are some of the things you'll be able to do during the summer
that you can't do now? Would you want to do those things as soon as possible? Why or
why not?

_____

_____

_____

_____

Name _____ Date _____

43. Imagine that you could create your perfect backyard pool, full of
all the pool games and toys you could ever want. Describe everything about this ideal pool.
Why would you enjoy it so much?

_____

_____

_____

_____

44. You have finally made it to the front of the line for the tallest and scariest waterslide in
the world. How do you feel as you get ready to jump in? What do you feel like as you
speedily propel forward?

_____

_____

_____

_____

Name _____ Date _____

45. How would summer be different for the following individuals
and why: firefighter, ice cream man, costumed baseball team mascot, and dog?

_____

_____

_____

_____

_____

46. Create a made-up story using the following words: heat wave, air conditioning, bubbly,
and laughter.

_____

_____

_____

_____

Name _____ Date _____

47. There are many different kinds of summer camps from soccer
camp to cooking camp. If you could attend one camp, even an imaginary one, what would
it be and why? What would your three favorite activities be there and why?

_____

_____

_____

_____

_____

48. One of the first summer jobs for many teenagers is as a counselor at a camp. Do you
think you'd enjoy being a counselor? Why or why not? What would you enjoy the most
about leading a bunch of kids through some fun summer games and why?

_____

_____

_____

_____

Name _____ Date _____

49. Your family is going on a long summer hike and you've brought
dozens of ways to cool you all down if you get too hot. What are the top three things you've packed to keep yourselves cool? Which one is the best and why?

_____

_____

_____

_____

50. You are a dry blade of grass during the dog days of summer. What kind of things might you be thinking about and why? How would you feel if it started to drizzle and why?

_____

_____

_____

_____

Name _____ Date _____

51. Imagine that you were forced to eat three meals completely made
out of pumpkins on the first day of fall. What different kinds of pumpkin foods might you
see? Would you get sick of pumpkins by the end? Why or why not?

_____

_____

_____

_____

52. What changes would need to be made if you were having a vegan Thanksgiving meal?
Which dishes that you enjoy the most would you have to skip? What are some meat- and
dairy-free foods that you might replace them with and why?

_____

_____

_____

_____

Name _____ Date _____

53. Describe what it might feel like to sit on your porch sipping a
warm apple cider watching the leaves fall from the trees. How would this feeling be
different from relaxing during the other seasons and why?

_____

_____

_____

_____

54. Cinnamon is one of the top spices of the season and can be used on anything from
gingersnap cookies to spiced drinks. What are your favorite foods that incorporate
cinnamon? Why do you think cinnamon reminds people of fall?

_____

_____

_____

_____

Name _____ Date _____

55. After a chilly day of leaf raking, what would be your ideal fall meal to warm you up? Would it be a soup or a stew? A baked lasagna or meatloaf? Explain your meal in great detail using all five senses to relay your experience.

_____

_____

_____

_____

56. The summer can be too hot for the oven, a problem not shared by the breezy and colder fall season. If you could create any oven-baked meal, what ingredients would it contain and why? Do you think it's necessary to follow a recipe when cooking? Why or why not?

_____

_____

_____

_____

Name _____ Date _____

57. Imagine that you have been given a choice between eating your family-cooking Thanksgiving meal or one cooked by a professional and famous chef. Would you pick the chef's meal even though you'd miss out on some of your favorite holiday tastes? Whose meal would you choose and why?

_____

_____

_____

_____

58. Which would you rather put on top of your fall meal: butter, gravy, or cranberry sauce and why? Would your parents approve of your hearty topping? Why or why not?

_____

_____

_____

_____

Name _____ Date _____

59. Create a conversation between a bowl of sweet potatoes and a bowl of mashed potatoes. What would these distantly related cousins have to talk about and why? Which of the two would you prefer at the dinner table and why?

_____

_____

_____

_____

_____

60. One of the major vegetables foods of fall is the mysterious squash. Imagine that you had to hunt for the origin of this strange delicacy for your dinner table. Where might your adventure take you and why?

_____

_____

_____

_____

Name _____ Date _____

61. You have placed a tracker on an acorn in an effort to find out
exactly where your backyard squirrels go during the day. After a squirrel takes the bait,
where does it go and why? Are you surprised to find out where the squirrel stashes its
goods? Why or why not?

_____

_____

_____

_____

62. Snow geese begin their migration trek of approximately 5,000 miles in the fall, heading
from the Arctic Tundra to the American south, east coast and southwest. What would it be
like to have to move far away every fall and winter? What would you miss about your
hometown during half of the year and why?

_____

_____

_____

_____

　　　　　　　　　　　　　　　　　　©2012 Build Creative Writing Ideas

Name _____ Date _____

63. Birds aren't the only animals that migrate in the fall, as monarch butterflies, humpback whales, and caribou all make the trek to warmer climates. Imagine that all three of these species made the trip to a warmer climate together. What challenges would they face and why?

_____

_____

_____

_____

_____

64. Animals getting ready to migrate start to change physically in the lead up to their long journey, storing more fat for their distant trips. How do humans change physically in the fall after the toasty summer months? Would they be able to handle a walk or jog as long as the birds can fly during the fall? Why or why not?

_____

_____

_____

_____

_____

Name _____ Date _____

65. Imagine that you were a crow getting ready to feast on some crops. All of a sudden, a creepy human-like creature, a scarecrow, has been posted in the middle of the field. What might you think of this straw-stuffed person? Would you avoid the vegetables? Why or why not?

_____

_____

_____

_____

66. After having all summer to hang with your pets, it's sad to leave them for the entire day when heading back to school. If you could take any of your pets with you to school, which ones would they be and why? Would your pet be able to behave itself? Why or why not?

_____

_____

_____

_____

Name _____ Date _____

67. While Thanksgiving and football go together, you never expected to see a group of 22 turkeys playing football in your backyard! Describe the fowl football game from the opening kickoff to the final drive. What do the turkeys look like during the competition and why?

_____

_____

_____

_____

68. The fox is often known as a sly and cunning animal. How would you describe the personalities of some other fall animals? Why do you think people try to give human characteristics to animals?

_____

_____

_____

_____

Name _____ Date _____

69. After hearing a knock on your window, you open it to find an owl waiting to give you some important life advice. What does the owl tell you? Do you believe the owl? What might happen if you try to put its advice into practice and why?

_____

_____

_____

_____

_____

70. If you could dress up as any animal for Halloween, what would it be and why? Would the animal fit with the fall season? Why or why not?

_____

_____

_____

_____

_____

Name _____ Date _____

71. Imagine that you came upon a pile of leaves that wasn't orange,
red, or yellow, but a strange fluorescent blue. What would you do about this glowing pile
of leaves and why would you do it?

_____

_____

_____

_____

72. Broccoli can be harvested in the fall after being planted in late summer. Do you enjoy
this healthy, green vegetable on its own or do you need to doctor it up with something
special? Why do you think many nutritious things don't taste great without some added
flavor?

_____

_____

_____

_____

Name _____ Date _____

73. Some plants use the length of daylight to figure out if they
should be creating flowers or shedding their leaves. If a flowering plant could talk during
the fall, what might it say about the changing season in relation to its daily routine and
why?

_____

_____

_____

_____

_____

74. Different pumpkin species can grow over 1,700 pounds if they are cared for well by
their farmers. What special tricks would you try if you were a pumpkin farmer to get your
orange squash to get that big? If you were successful, what would you do with such a huge
pumpkin?

_____

_____

_____

_____

_____

Name _____ Date _____

75. Fall gourds of all shapes and sizes can be used to decorate the outside and inside of your house. Imagine that you were given 10,000 gourds to really bring the fall spirit to every inch of your home. What would your parents think of your design and why?

_____

_____

_____

_____

76. Visiting a fall pumpkin patch is an exciting time for the whole family. Imagine that all fruits and vegetables grew on the ground in a patch. Which natural delicacies would you and your family go picking and why?

_____

_____

_____

_____

Name _____ Date _____

77. Wheat, rye, barley, and other grains can be harvested in the fall or winter. Imagine that you were allergic to wheat and other grains. What foods might you not be able to eat? How do you think you'd replace those foods in your diet?

_____

_____

_____

_____

78. Apples can be used for pie, cider, and many other fall treats. What do you think is the best use of apples and why? Would your family members agree with you? Why or why not?

_____

_____

_____

_____

Name _____ Date _____

79. What would it be like if another fruit or vegetable replaced the pumpkin as the supreme symbol of fall? How might some fall traditions change and why?

_____

_____

_____

_____

_____

80. Festivals related to harvesting vegetable, grain, and fruit crops are celebrated throughout the world. Why do you think the harvest is thought to be so important? Do you think that the importance of the harvest will decrease in the future? Why or why not?

_____

_____

_____

_____

Name _____ Date _____

81. The green color of leaves is the result of the chemical chlorophyll, which becomes limited during the fall as a result of less sunshine. Imagine that you changed color if you didn't get enough sun. Which seasons might cause you to transform? What color would you change into and why?

_____

_____

_____

_____

_____

82. Without the green chlorophyll, leaves begin to show bright colors as a result of other chemicals called carotenoids and anthocyanins. What is your favorite fall leaf color and why? Would you paint your house or room that color? Why or why not?

_____

_____

_____

_____

Name _____ Date _____

83. Trees use this season to suck up the last bit of sugar and other
nutrients from their leaves before they fall off. Have you ever licked the bottom of a bowl
or cup to enjoy the last bit of food or drink? What might your parents think of your
manners if you did and why?

_____

_____

_____

_____

_____

84. Plants are also able to put some of their waste products into leaves, effectively taking
out the trash by dumping the leaves during the fall. While it's OK for trees to drop their
trash, why is it important for you to humans to pick up after themselves? What are some
examples of trash you've seen that haven't been properly thrown away?

_____

_____

_____

_____

Name _____ Date _____

85. Another reason for trees to get rid of their leaves is for the plant to conserve its water during the upcoming dry winter. Why might it be important for humans to conserve water? What are some ways that you can conserve water in your house?

_____

_____

_____

_____

86. Not all trees lose their leaves during the fall. Evergreens keep their small, sharp needles all year round. Imagine how you'd feel if everyone around you was changing while you stayed exactly the same. Would you try to fit in? Why or why not?

_____

_____

_____

_____

Name _____ Date _____

87. Fall is host to one of the biggest meteor showers of the year with
the November Leonids. Create a conversation between two meteors shooting across the
sky looking down at your and your family during the shower. What might these comet dust
particles have to say about you and why?

_____

_____

_____

_____

88. Flu season begins during the fall and scientists use chicken eggs to create the vaccines
against the infectious viral disease. Do you think it's necessary to protect yourself against
the flu virus? Would your parents agree with you? Why or why not?

_____

_____

_____

_____

Name _____ Date _____

89. The harvest moon is the name given to the final full moon before
the fall season officially begins. This moon gives farmers the opportunity to work through
the night to harvest their crops. What are some ways in which a full moon could help you
during the night?

_____

_____

_____

_____

90. Imagine that humans had leaves instead of hair. How would you style your bushy head
and what colors would your leaves change into during the fall? What would you do during
the winter without any hair or leaves and why?

_____

_____

_____

_____

Name _____ Date _____

91. As the season of Halloween, fall can be quite frightening. What
is the most scared you've ever been? What caused it and how did you overcome your fear?

_____

_____

_____

_____

_____

92. How do you think your fears will change as you get older? Will you be afraid of more
or fewer things and why?

_____

_____

_____

_____

Name _____ Date _____

93. What are some of the sounds of fall? Why aren't these noises
usually found during the summer or spring? How do these sounds make you feel when you
hear them and why?

_____

_____

_____

_____

94. You have been hired to write and direct a Hollywood movie centered on fall and
people falling in love. Who would star in it, where would you film it, and how successful
do you think it would be?

_____

_____

_____

_____

Name _____ Date _____

95. You and your family are hosting a foreign exchange student who comes from a hot climate that doesn't experience much fall weather. What would it be like for him to see the leaves falling for the first time and why? Would he enjoy it? Why or why not?

_____

_____

_____

_____

96. What would fall be like if we lived in a world without trees and falling leaves? What else might be different about this strange world and why?

_____

_____

_____

_____

Name _____ Date _____

97. While trees have no more use for leaves in the fall, there are plenty of things that we can use them for. What are some uses for leaves to lighten your raking load? Which is your favorite use and why?

_____

_____

_____

_____

98. After a delivery mistake, there are 1,000 pumpkins sitting in your front yard. How will you and your family deal with all these pumpkins? Would you ever get sick of endless pumpkin pies and cheesecakes? Why or why not?

_____

_____

_____

_____

Name _____ Date _____

99. Imagine that every day of fall included a feast as big as Thanksgiving. What would happen to the fitness level of your family? Which Thanksgiving foods would you get sick of and why?

_____

_____

_____

_____

_____

100. You have been handed a treasure map to the greatest fall treasure of all: a secret stash of the tastiest Thanksgiving recipes in existence. Who will you enlist to help you find the treasure? Describe your journey from beginning to end.

_____

_____

_____

_____

_____

Name _____ Date _____

101. There's nothing like a hot bowl of soup on a chilly winter's day. What other hot foods tend to warm you up during the coldest seasons? Which is your favorite toasty food and why?

_____

_____

_____

_____

_____

102. Imagine that you and your family are hiking up the side of a snowy mountain. While taking a small break, you take out a bag of trail mix. What kinds of nuts, seeds, and other items might you find in your energizing snack pack? Why might you need energy to keep going up the side of the mountain?

_____

_____

_____

_____

Name _____ Date _____

103. You have invited all of your friends over for a winter chili
cook-off! What ingredients do you use in your chili? What does your chili taste like? Do
you win? Why or why not?

_____

_____

_____

_____

104. The perfect hot chocolate has much more than a simple mix combined with hot water.
What other treats would you put into your ideal hot chocolate to heat you up after a long
day of playing? Would your parents approve of your recipe? Why or why not?

_____

_____

_____

_____

Name _____ Date _____

105. While you might wish that a warm plate of cookies or brownies
was waiting for you every day after school, it certainly isn't the healthiest choice. What might happen if you ate brownies all winter long? What are some more nutritious choices and why?

_____

_____

_____

_____

_____

106. Your parents have put you in charge of making a delicious, hot winter meal of macaroni and cheese. Will you come up with your own recipe or use the stuff from the box? How long would it take you and why? Will your parents appreciate your efforts? Why or why not?

_____

_____

_____

_____

_____

Name _____ Date _____

107. On a trip out of town, your parents have given you permission
to make a waffle in the hotel's waffle maker and to put any toppings on it you want. What
toppings do you choose and what does your breakfast taste like?

_____

_____

_____

_____

108. Imagine that you've been shrunk down to the size of a raisin! As you swim around
your bowl of morning oatmeal trying to get your parents' attention, you decide to go
exploring. Where do you go next and how do you get yourself out of this tiny
predicament?

_____

_____

_____

_____

Name _____ Date _____

109. Some of the best winter meals come from the slow cooker, which can take hours and hours to use effectively. Imagine that you had to make a meal that took more than five hours. What would you do with your time while you waited for it to cook and why?

_____

_____

_____

_____

_____

110. What is your family's go-to meal during the winter? Why do you think your parents cook it so often during the chilliest months? Would you change this frequent meal to another one if you had a choice? Why or why not?

_____

_____

_____

_____

Name _____ Date _____

111. Imagine that you and your family members were polar bears
instead of humans. How would your usual routine change? What would you do for food?
Would it be tough living in the snow? Why or why not?

_____

_____

_____

_____

_____

112. Some birds fly south during the winter to find warmer areas of the country. What are
some reasons they might migrate? Would your family ever consider taking the few months
of winter on a warm island? Why or why not?

_____

_____

_____

_____

Name _____ Date _____

113. Birds aren't the only organisms that migrate, as beetles and worms burrow deep into the soil to spend the winter in a warmer environment. What is the warmest part of your house? Do you ever cuddle up in it to keep toasty on a cold day? Why or why not?

_____

_____

_____

_____

114. A frog can hibernate during the winter at the bottom of a pond underneath the frozen water. How would your winter be different if you spent three straight months hiding and sleeping? What are some of the things you might miss and why?

_____

_____

_____

_____

Name _____ Date _____

115. During hibernation, bears can sleep as long as six months, during which time they don't eat, sleep, or use the bathroom. What would happen if you fell asleep for six straight months? What kind of things might you miss? How would you catch up and why?

_____

_____

_____

_____

116. Squirrels and other animals stockpile nuts during the warmer months so they have food all winter long. Imagine that your family couldn't go shopping during the snowy season and had to buy everything beforehand. What foods might you have to skip? What foods would you eat all the time and why?

_____

_____

_____

_____

Name _____ Date _____

117. Some insects actually change into different forms during the winter to stay warmer and safer. Imagine that you could change into something else during the coldest months of the year. What would you change into and why? What would your parents think of your transformation?

_____

_____

_____

_____

118. You and your friends are using tracks in the snow to figure out what animals have been running around in your backyard. What do the tracks look like and what animals do you assume have been there? How do you find more evidence to prove your hypothesis? Are you correct? Why or why not?

_____

_____

_____

_____

Name _____ Date _____

119. Animals may grow warmer fur or have their fur change colors
to match snow during the winter. What are some ways that you adapt to the cold
temperatures?

_____

_____

_____

_____

120. If you could be any winter animal, which one would you choose and why? What
would be some of your new challenges as this icy season animal? What would you enjoy
the most as this animal and why?

_____

_____

_____

_____

Name _____ Date _____

121. In the months leading up to winter, plants develop cold hardiness, which allows them to handle the upcoming colder months. Imagine that your skin and body changed during the winter. How would it change and how would it improve your resistance to the cold?

_____

_____

_____

_____

122. Another winter preparation step for plants includes not growing during the winter. Why might plants be more vulnerable to the cold if they kept growing? What might happen if you gave plants a lot of food right before the winter and why?

_____

_____

_____

_____

Name _____ Date _____

123. You and your family have taken up winter vegetable farming, harvesting veggies like broccoli, Brussels sprouts, cabbage, kale, and onions. What might be difficult about harvesting these crops in the winter? Would you enjoy the dishes made from these vegetables? Why or why not?

_____

_____

_____

_____

_____

124. Annuals are plants that live only one year, die off at the end of summer and then leave their seeds to survive the harsh winter months. What would it be like to live an entire lifetime in only one year? What are some things annuals miss out on by only living one year?

_____

_____

_____

_____

_____

Name _____ Date _____

125. Some seeds can live over one hundred years buried deep in cold soil before they germinate. How tough do you think pregnancy would have been on your mom if you were in her womb for twice or three times as long and why?

_____

_____

_____

_____

126. Trees that live near the Arctic change during the winter to produce sap that is extremely sweet and sugary. Not only does this keep the tree from freezing, but humans can harvest the sap to use on pancakes. What would it be like to take the syrupy sap directly from one of these trees and why?

_____

_____

_____

_____

Name _____ Date _____

127. Like squirrels, some plants start storing food in the form of
bulbs and tubers during the fall to prep for the winter. Create a conversation between two
plants during the winter, bored of eating the same old stored food all winter long. What do
they talk about and why?

_____

_____

_____

_____

128. Some trees have adapted to hold off budding new leaves until they can tell that winter
is over. Do you think that winter feels different from spring? How is it different? How
might a tree be able to feel the difference between the two seasons?

_____

_____

_____

_____

　　　　　　　　　　　　　　　　　　　　　　©2012 Build Creative Writing Ideas

Name _____ Date _____

129. Conifers, including pine trees, make perfect Christmas trees
because their leaves don't fall off before winter. Why might their leaves be able to survive
the harsh temperatures of winter? How would you compare the appearance of a pine tree to
a tree without any leaves?

_____

_____

_____

_____

130. What are some ways in which winter plants and winter animals could work together
for survival? Why would it be a good idea for them to help each other out?

_____

_____

_____

_____

Name _____ Date _____

131. Because of the way the Earth tilts in relation to the sun, winter on one side of the world would actually be the same months as summer on the other side. How would your life be different if January was one of the hottest months and why?

_____

_____

_____

_____

_____

132. If you lived at the North Pole, you would experience 24 hours straight of darkness on the first day of winter. What would you do differently if you were sun-free for an entire day? Would you miss the daylight? Why or why not?

_____

_____

_____

_____

Name _____ Date _____

133. Winter storms are the result of both warm and cold air masses, which is why some of the weather is rain while some of it is snow. What are some of the challenges of a rainy and snowy winter storm? What might your parents tell you to do during such a storm?

_____

_____

_____

_____

_____

134. In March 1993, a winter superstorm led to snow, wind, rain and low temperatures in 26 different states. Imagine what would happen if a winter storm were to affect the entire country? How might your life be affected and why?

_____

_____

_____

_____

Name _____ Date _____

135. While it seems really cold at 0 degrees Fahrenheit, there have
been winter temperatures recorded that are 100 degrees below Fahrenheit! What clothing
might you need to wear to protect yourself from such cold temperatures? Why wouldn't
you want to live in an area that gets that cold?

_____

_____

_____

_____

136. Snowflakes grow into beautiful six-sided crystals because of the way that water looks
at a microscopic level. Imagine that you could shrink down to the size of a snowflake;
what would it look like from this perspective and why?

_____

_____

_____

_____

Name _____ Date _____

137. The body shivers when it's cold because the brain sends signals to the muscles to move around quickly to generate heat. What are some other ways that you generate heat when you're cold? Why does moving around keep you warmer than simply sitting in the snow?

_____

_____

_____

_____

_____

138. Wearing a hat is important during the winter because approximately 50 percent of body heat can be lost through the head. Imagine you could make your own winter hat from scratch. What would the hat look like and how would it keep you warm during the coldest months?

_____

_____

_____

_____

Name _____ Date _____

139. Frostbite and hypothermia can occur if you stay out in the cold too long without proper clothing on. What are some other winter dangers that can happen if you don't take safety precautions? How can you best stay safe during winter and why?

_____

_____

_____

_____

140. Driving a car during the winter is extremely dangerous because there is much less friction between the car's tires and the road. What might it be like to drive a car on an icy road? What things would you need to do to be as safe as possible and why?

_____

_____

_____

_____

Name _____ Date _____

141. You've been chosen to lead a winter expedition in the North
Pole on the first day of winter. With harsh elements and no sunlight, how will you succeed
in your mission? What tools would you need, who would you take to help you, and why?

_____

_____

_____

_____

142. Create a conversation between two sleigh dogs on your expedition. Do they enjoy
working for you? Why or why not? If they had the choice, would they be running at the
North Pole or somewhere else and why?

_____

_____

_____

_____

Name _____ Date _____

143. There's nothing like burrowing under a large pile of blankets on a chilly night. Write a story about your family all snuggling into one bed covered in blankets. Describe the blankets in great detail as well as how they make you feel.

_____

_____

_____

_____

_____

144. In the not-too-distant past, families had to make their own clothing and blankets to protect against the bitter cold of winter. What kinds of clothes would your family make and why? How would you contribute to the process and why?

_____

_____

_____

_____

Name _____ Date _____

145. Imagine what it would have been like to get around in your neighborhood during a snowstorm before cars were invented. What would you do if you needed to get to school or work? What other conveniences might you not have that far in the past?

_____

_____

_____

_____

146. Will it be easier to deal with snow and ice 100 or more years in the future? What inventions might your generation and future generations create to take the bite out of the season? Which would be your favorite to use and why?

_____

_____

_____

_____

Name _____ Date _____

147. What are some activities that you love to do during the winter?
Which is your favorite and where would you do it if you had the choice? Why might it be tougher to do that activity in a different season?

_____

_____

_____

_____

148. What are the extra chores you might have to take on during the winter? Which is the easiest one and why? Which is the most difficult and why? Do you have fun doing any winter chores? Why or why not?

_____

_____

_____

_____

Name _____ Date _____

149. Some parents get very overprotective during the winter. Would your parents fit that description? Why or why not? How do you think your parents acted during a snowstorm when they were your age and why?

_____

_____

_____

_____

150. You have been selected to design a completely winter-proof house. What would it look like, what materials would you use, and who would live in it? Would the house be tough to live in during the summer? Why or why not?

_____

_____

_____

_____

Name _____ Date _____

151. Many spring meals consist of fresh fruits and vegetables. If you
had a choice, would you rather eat something fresh or a food from a box or can and why?
Is your favorite spring meal fresh or processed?

_____

_____

_____

_____

_____

152. In honor of spring, you're hosting a party at your house with all of your friends. What
foods will you put on the menu to both celebrate spring and impress your guests? What are
some foods you absolutely wouldn't choose and why?

_____

_____

_____

_____

_____

Name _____ Date _____

153. One of the simplest spring desserts is combining fresh strawberries with whipped cream. Would you say that you have simple tastes or that you like things with a lot of different flavors and why? Would you make a good food taster? Why or why not?

_____

_____

_____

_____

_____

154. You have been chosen to create the best and most nutritious salad the world has ever seen. Where will you go looking for these tasty spring ingredients? Would you eat the salad yourself? Why or why not?

_____

_____

_____

_____

Name _____ Date _____

155. The spring is the season for the incredible, edible egg! The happiest and healthiest chickens tend to make the tastiest eggs. How hard do you think it would be to treat a chicken right? What steps might you have to take to make sure your chicken was the best she could be and why?

_____

_____

_____

_____

156. Once you have the eggs from your healthy, happy chicken, what will you do with them? What are five different ways you could use eggs in meals? Which would be your favorite and why?

_____

_____

_____

_____

Name _____ Date _____

157. Your family has been entered into a fruit pie baking contest and all of you have to help. Which baking task would each of you take and why? What kind of spring pie might you make and why?

_____

_____

_____

_____

158. Some of the best spring seasonings include mint, oregano, rosemary, cilantro, and dill. What are your favorite herbs that you or your parents use to spice up your food? Why is it important to use herbs instead of just salt and ketchup?

_____

_____

_____

_____

Name _____ Date _____

159. Fresh cheese straight from the dairy farmer is a wonderful
spring treat. What are your favorite uses for cheese? Would you rather have it on a
sandwich, a pizza, or on something else? How do you think fresh cheese would be
different from processed cheese and why?

_____

_____

_____

_____

160. Imagine that you were a rabbit running about the neighborhood during the spring.
What kind of vegetables and plants would you look for to eat? Do you think you would be
healthier as a human if you ate like that rabbit sometimes? Why or why not?

_____

_____

_____

_____

Name _____ Date _____

161. Many animals have their babies in the spring because of longer days and plentiful amounts of food. Imagine that you found a lost baby animal and had to take care of it until you found its family. What would the animal be? What would you have to do to take care of it? Would you enjoy being an animal parent? Why or why not?

_____

_____

_____

_____

_____

162. Birds sing beautiful songs to find their mates for the spring. Do you think this is a good process for picking someone to spend your life with? Why or why not? If you were a bird, would you add any other things to look for? Why or why not?

_____

_____

_____

_____

Name _____ Date _____

163. How do you think humans would be different if they had to lay eggs during the spring and sit on them until they hatched? Would your parents take turns on the eggs? Would you have to sit on the egg of a baby brother or sister? Why or why not?

_____

_____

_____

_____

164. The many migrating birds that left during the fall and winter return home during the spring to find mates and have babies. Why do you think the birds don't just stay in one warm place? What might be some reasons they feel the need to travel hundreds or thousands of miles twice a year?

_____

_____

_____

_____

Name _____ Date _____

165. Hibernating animals like hedgehogs, bats, bears, and squirrels begin to wake up from their long slumber during the spring. How do you feel after you've taken a long nap? What might you need to do to completely wake up? How would that compare to a hibernating bear and why?

_____

_____

_____

_____

166. Even though they're cute, rabbits can wreak havoc on your backyard garden as they look for food to eat. Imagine that you have been hired as the guard of your parents' garden. What would you do to scare the rabbits away from your parents' carrots? Would you be successful? Why or why not?

_____

_____

_____

_____

Name _____ Date _____

167. Monarch butterflies take part in a wild yearlong journey including a move from Mexico to Texas and Florida at the beginning of the summer to lay eggs on the milkweed plant, the only plant monarch caterpillars can eat. What would happen to these butterflies if the milkweed went extinct and why?

_____

_____

_____

_____

168. After the trip to Mexico and the southwestern United States, these butterflies can go as far north as Canada during the spring and summer before the cycle continues. What would it be like to be one of these globetrotting butterflies? Would you enjoy all the traveling? Why or why not?

_____

_____

_____

_____

Name _____ Date _____

169. Upon noticing hundreds of salamanders trying to cross a nearby street to get to a spring mating pond, you and your friends decide to build a tunnel to keep the amphibians safe. How do you get this tunnel approved? What do you use to create the tunnel? What is the end result and why?

_____

_____

_____

_____

_____

170. While mating seasons occur during the spring in most areas, animals in tropical climates don't stick to one particular time of year. Why do you think that is? What would you do differently than you do now if you lived on a tropical island and why?

_____

_____

_____

_____

Name _____ Date _____

171. The beautiful blooming flowers of spring include daisies, irises, and lilies. What would it be like if humans could bloom? What would they look like and why?

_____

_____

_____

_____

_____

172. One blooming flower that can be considered a weed is the dandelion. How do you think this green and yellow plant spread itself throughout the whole world? Are there any plants you'd rather were as common as the dandelion? If so, what plants and why?

_____

_____

_____

_____

Name _____ Date _____

173. While some people don't like them, dandelions have many helpful properties and have been used in medicine and for coffee substitutes. What is an example of something in your life that has many different uses? What do you use it for and why?

_____

_____

_____

_____

174. Imagine that you have been invited to a festival to watch the blooming of a really ugly spring plant. What would the plant look like? Why would everybody be celebrating it if it was so strange-looking?

_____

_____

_____

_____

Name _____ Date _____

175. While some flowers need to be planted months in advance to flower in the spring, many trees need to be tended to for years or decades to reach their full potential. Do you think it would be worth it to care for a plant for more than a year? Why or why not?

_____

_____

_____

_____

_____

176. You are a small insect living on a plant in a huge spring garden. What kind of plant would you want to live on and why? How would your insect life be different from your human life and why?

_____

_____

_____

_____

Name _____ Date _____

177. Have you ever planted a seed to watch it grow? If so, did it turn out how you expected? Why or why not? If not, imagine that a seed you planted turned out to be something wildly different than you thought it was. Describe the mystery plant in great detail.

_____

_____

_____

_____

_____

178. Spring is the best season for strawberries to get the freshest and juiciest berries. Create a conversation between two strawberries discussing how they hope to be used by humans. What are some of their options other than simply being eaten?

_____

_____

_____

_____

Name _____ Date _____

179. Naval oranges are best picked during the spring. What is the
freshest orange juice you've ever had? What would you have to do to get it even more
fresh? Would the juice taste different if the fruit came straight from the tree? Why or why
not?

_____

_____

_____

_____

_____

180. Imagine that you could plant an entire farm of your favorite spring fruits. Which ones
would you choose and why? Would you want to take part in the farming yourself or would
you rather just eat the fruit and skip the work and why?

_____

_____

_____

_____

_____

Name _____ Date _____

181. Spring and the other three seasons are the result of the Earth spinning while tilted at 23.5 degrees. What would it be like if you couldn't walk around straight because you were slightly tilted all day long? What challenges would you face in everyday tasks and why?

_____

_____

_____

_____

182. The constellations Virgo and Leo are visible at night during the spring but they can't be seen at all during the fall. Why is it that we see different constellations in different seasons? Do you enjoy stargazing? Why or why not?

_____

_____

_____

_____

Name _____ Date _____

183. As the spring days get longer, plants start to wake up from their
winter slumber by forming buds and growing again. What are some changes that you
undergo during the spring? How would those changes be different during an unseasonably
chilly and winter-like spring?

_____

_____

_____

_____

184. Create a conversation between two sprouting seeds in the ground. What do these
soon-to-be fully grown plants have to discuss? What are some of the challenges of being a
seed that they might be worried about and why?

_____

_____

_____

_____

Name _____ Date _____

185. Imagine that plants needed something different from sunlight
and water to grow. What would these new plant requirements be and why? Would it be
easier or harder to grow plants with these different needs and why?

_____

_____

_____

_____

186. As the flowers bloom during the spring, bees move from plant to plant helping the
plants to reproduce through the process of pollination. Are you afraid of bees? Why or why
not? Since bees are so helpful to flowers, do you think flowers are scared of bees as well?
Why or why not?

_____

_____

_____

_____

Name _____ Date _____

187. Even though bees are scary, they are necessary to help the growth of a lot of the food we eat. What do you think would happen if all of the bees got sick and couldn't fly? What might happen to the plants and why?

_____

_____

_____

_____

188. Springtime isn't just about plants growing, as kids tend to grow slightly faster in the spring compared with other seasons. Imagine that you had a big growth spurt all season long. How tall would you grow and what kind of changes would you need to make? What would your parents think about your spurt and why?

_____

_____

_____

_____

Name _____ Date _____

189. Extra rain mixed with melting snow can cause floods during the
spring. What would your family do if it started to flood in your neighborhood? How would
you make sure that you could stay safe with the large amount of water whooshing by?

_____

_____

_____

_____

190. As flowers and bees spread pollen, humans can start having allergic reactions such as
sneezing and coughing. Seasonal allergies affect millions of people. Imagine that you were
allergic to something you enjoyed doing or eating. How would you cope? What would you
change to try to replace this enjoyable thing and why?

_____

_____

_____

_____

Name _____ Date _____

191. While your parents are out of town on a second honeymoon, you have been asked to tend to the spring garden. What kinds of tasks might you need to do to keep it healthy? Will you be successful? Why or why not?

_____

_____

_____

_____

192. When spring break comes around, it's important to clear your head for the last leg of school. What is the best way for you to relax and why? Do you usually feel relaxed upon your return? Why or why not?

_____

_____

_____

_____

Name _____ Date _____

193. Spring cleaning is upon us and your parents have locked you in your room until it's completely clean. What area would you have to tackle first? How would you feel while you were cleaning? How would you feel when you're all done and why?

_____

_____

_____

_____

_____

194. Will you think about spring cleaning differently when you have your own house in the future? Why or why not? What will be the toughest party of tidying your own pad and why?

_____

_____

_____

_____

Name _____ Date _____

195. You have climbed to the top of the tallest tree in the forest, giving yourself the best view in town. How would this view be different in the spring than it would in other seasons and why?

_____

_____

_____

_____

_____

196. How would the spring view from the top of a tree be different than the view of a furry mouse on the ground? Which of you would have a better view and why? How might the mouse feel about its view and why?

_____

_____

_____

_____

Name _____ Date _____

197. Describe the perfect spring day running around playing with your friends. What activities would you do and why? Where would you play and with whom? How would the day make you feel and why?

_____

_____

_____

_____

198. How would you spend your ideal spring day if nobody was around? Do you think your activities would be the same as other people who are alone during the spring? Why or why not? Would you rather have the alone day or the day with friends and why?

_____

_____

_____

_____

Name _____ Date _____

199. What is some music that reminds you of the spring? How is that music different from the music of the other seasons? Which season has your favorite music and why?

_____

_____

_____

_____

200. You have been commissioned to write a song about spring. What would some of the lyrics be and why? What other songs might your song sound like and how would your song be used?

_____

_____

_____

_____

Extra Page

Name _____ Date _____

_____

_____

_____

_____

_____

_____

_____

_____

_____

_____

_____

ABOUT THE AUTHOR

Bryan Cohen is a writer, actor and director who grew up in Dresher, Pennsylvania just outside of Philadelphia. He graduated from the University of North Carolina at Chapel Hill with degrees in English and Dramatic Art along with a minor in Creative Writing. His books on writing prompts and writing motivation have sold over 15,000 copies and they include *1,000 Creative Writing Prompts: Ideas for Blogs, Scripts, Stories and More, 1,000 Character Writing Prompts: Villains, Heroes and Hams for Scripts, Stories and More, 500 Writing Prompts for Kids: First Grade through Fifth Grade, 1,000 Character Writing Prompts: Villains, Heroes and Hams for Scripts, Stories and More* and *The Post-College Guide to Happiness*. Cohen continues to produce and perform plays and films in between his books and freelance writing work. He lives in Chicago.

Made in the USA
Lexington, KY
10 June 2014